Dominique Hecq

Endgame with No Ending

SurVision Books

First published in 2023 by
SurVision Books
Dublin, Ireland
Reggio di Calabria, Italy
www.survisionmagazine.com

Copyright © Dominique Hecq, 2023

Design © SurVision Books, 2023

ISBN: 978-1-912963-42-3

This book is in copyright. No part of this publication may be reproduced, stored in a retrieval system, or transmitted in any form or by any means without the prior permission in writing from the publisher.

Acknowledgements

Grateful acknowledgement is made to the editors of the following, in which some of these poems, or versions of them, originally appeared:

Axon; Aesthetica Creative Award 2022 Anthology (ed. Oz Hardwick); *Décision; Not Very Quiet; Play: An Anthology of the Joanne Burns Microlit Award 2023* (ed. Cassandra Atherton); *Rabbit; Shadows and Tall Trees Anthology* (ed. Mark Davidson); *Tiny Spoon; Travel: An Anthology of the Joanne Burns Microlit Award 2022* (ed. Cassandra Atherton); *Western Humanities Review*.

Special thanks to The ScAN/AAWP Neuroscience and Creative Writing Collaboration Project for commissioning work in response to three digital images of the human brain. Also, huge thanks to the community of writers and readers from the Prose Poetry Project at IPSI, and to Catherine Clover for inviting me to participate in 'Wild Energies: Live Materials', a symposium held at the Creative Research into Sound Arts Practice department at the University of Arts, London.

CONTENTS

Travelogue Dalí	7
Cursive	8
The Entombment	9
Anaphora	10
Confession of a Bookworm	12
Borges and I	13
Ariadne Dreams of a New Relativity	14
Archives of the Future	15
Cross-swell Heisenberg	16
Aseptic Perception	17
Twinklewinkalling	18
Ekphrastic Still	19
Con Brio	20
How It Is	21
Champagne Supernova, Taché	22
Whimsical	23
The Edge Land of Dreams	24
Rrose Sélavy	25
Letter to a Bride to Be	26
Magritte's Gravestone	27
A Haunting	28
Less Is a Bore	29
Π	30
Telescopic	32
Endgame with No Ending	33
Notes	34

*we find ourselves
part of the tree of cod es
Reality is as thin as paper*

—Jonathan Foer

Travelogue Dalí

A procession of words legible as the horizon would be at a withheld point, withheld time: a heart-scratched itinerary inside a seagull's gullet. Once a mermaid cavorting with Botticelli's Venus, you are now a mere pinprick principle vying with toxins, paperclips, peanuts, cigarette buts, skeins of silk, stirrups, socks, glyphs, icicles, exoskeletons, nails, cuneiforms, marbles and jellyfish. You grit your teeth. Select a monocle. Meticulously reconstruct the contortionist's honeymoon: wedding ring, lobster, credit card, hourglass, steel mesh, Bible, harp, condom, cross, knife, eyeball, scarf, Botox, blubber, Xanax, a print of Millet's *Angelus,* and an alternative-history book set in Nazified France and titled *The Grand Alliance.* You invoke the spirit of the praying mantis. A scenario begins to emerge. You reconnect with the pin part of your existential principle. Spellbound and tele-exiled, you fly from Melbourne to Nice where two thousand bloods run, filtering fables from far ago. Where all is dark shaken, veil over mass exodus. Where corpuscular clouds twine the sky and bells every time unhinged toll for a soul. 'Tis done. You autograph your script. Unrushed, the millennial eagle soars in the pixelated dusk. God haemorrhages. You recede into cerise smoke.

Cursive

I hate Times Roman. Love Chancery Cursive. Love chance. Love gallivanting around the word. Chancery Cursive captures how the hand runs across the page. How letters get excited at the beginning of a piece. How they flourish in movement. Cursive lids the light. Echoes mind-chambers and smells of honeysuckle. It gives body to sans-serif. Chancery Cursive takes off like writing in which the letters are joined and formed rapidly without lifting the nib of your pen, from the French *cursif*, from the Medieval Latin *cursivus*, from the Latin *cursus*, all run-running words. Even the past participle *currere*, meaning to run, from the Indo-European root **kers* that always reminds me what a curse a running hand is. Chancery Cursive is a marathon runner. It is tall and lean. It lives vertically, although it does embrace the wind in its course. It thrives on air, blood and water, seeds and nuts. Breeds dream-begotten strokes, forms, letters. *See how they run away from Times Roman.*

The Entombment

In the sky-blubbering sea stands entombed a dead alive elephant with sawn tusks under a dome of azure ice. The elephant looks through me with pecked at lapis lazuli eyes. Its accusatory stare reaches not only beyond the sea but also beyond the horizon that bleeds into violet stars strewn on the crust of the earth. This could be a still from a Disney cartoon. A photograph from *Fantasia after the Apocalypse*. A hologram portending impending doom. I want to coax out the blue. But it would take days to knead and press and squeeze a dough of powdered lapis, wax, resin and linseed oil. Besides, the water is frozen and I have no wood ash. I'm Queen Boadicea dunked in woad cobalt oxide wailing for a child I never had. I'm a stone Buddha facing Ganesh. I'm Kubla Kahn turning Midnight Blue. I'm a petrified bird of paradise shooting through the Anthropocene. The elephant charges. Waves crash. I'm the Mount Lebanon Blue butterfly smashed to smithereens. I'm dancing matter that does not matter. I'm ultramarine. Utter darkness. I'm a mind unminding itself. Entombing itself. I'm *Ash in this sunless sea sinking in tumult to a lifeless ocean*. I'm molecules of oxygen and hydrogen. I'm particles of dust in frozen H_2O. In this inky *pleasure dome with caves of ice*. I'm nameless.

Anaphora

The day without ceremony begins with blackbirds. Bells unhinged. Silence is an air bubble breaking. I move amid feathers beneath unbuttoned eyes. Light. Unmusical yet rhythmical sounds echo in the room. Voyce, face closed, touches the fugue of language. Silence is an air bubble breaking, I say. A quizzical expression beclouds her face. Laughter bursts in her breath. I touch the sky. Phonemes cut the air. Images, words, letters cascade. Tropisms rustle inside. Voyce and I, one and the other conjoined in the obsolete art of conversing. All is a wave of sound. Tide of noise. Unmusical yet rhythmical. A horn blast. Funny how the world seeps through the conversation. Cracks meaning. Sorry, that's not what I meant at all. Images, words, letters cascade. Litter the floor (the forward movement of speech is associative rhythm, connection, disconnection, repetition, disconnection, disrupted flux *tending-not-tending-to-hemiola.*) Tropisms rustle inside. Voyce and I, one and the other conjoined in this disappearing life. We trail off into silence. I can be played on any instrument I, or Voyce, then says: *Shh Shh Shh.* Did you **hear**? Hum. High and eerie keening. Voyce is not a person of many words. Her face closed, she touches the fugue of language before language. A fractal tune floats through the air. I gesture towards the piano. Puffing exhalations, chiming, puffing exhalations. Voyce sits down at the instrument. Rip tide of sound. I am speechless—*one-**and**, two-**and**, three-**and**, four-**and**, five-**and**, six-**and**...* Her hands move so swiftly and fluidly on the keyboard of language before the fugue of language it's hypnotic. Black birds white birds black fish white fish black frogs white frogs. And winding up the performance *one-**and**, two-**and**,* *three-**and**, four-**and**, five-**and**, six-**and** seven **and*** Voyce finishes with a parodic flourish. Wow! We glide inwards towards the very centre of Escher's *Verbum.*

Confession of a Bookworm

The book is in a cardboard cover marked Fragile. I tenderly lift the volume out of its dogeared case. Scraps of leather binding and confettied paper fall on the floor in a cloud of organic matter. I wish I were an alchemist, a botanist, or a physician, but my eyes naturally turn to calligraphy and flashes of colour. I kneel down. Sneeze. Finger the powder when out of the blue the Abbé Raynal storms into the library and screams: *malheureuse*! My fingers are red and, as I try to rub the colour off the palms of my hands, grow red. *Malheureuse! Dactylopius coccus* holds the secret of cochineal. You will be tried for treason to the sound of Spanish thundering cannons and French trumpets. You will receive angry salutes from twenty-four pounders. And you will burn among phials and flasks and cases of books.

Borges and I

I sit by the opening of this labyrinthine library between a dark angel and his gossamer-clad acolyte. I point my boat out to sea, clutching memories of life and love, only to return to the shore. Its slippery pebbles, white and porous, soon grey with soot and red with rust: these bleed in trails of flickering flames. Borges's hair is on fire. He says poets have to remain with the concrete image. All language, I roll on, is abstract. Take the word rock: it's both more and less than an actual rock. He says all we could ever work with is the experience of the five senses. I say there are more than five senses. Thoughts, I say, are sensed and the movement of thought is perceptible; there are pre-verbal and pre-conceptual experiences. My skin is burning. Look, I snap, gesturing to the window: hail / flung at us // drops of water / trickling down the glass // sleet / refracting / baubles of light // hung in the sky's vault // rocks / fire-spiking // your mind's birded flight. And equally ready to fly, says Borges: words peck at your skull, their beak punctuating the long sentence of memory on the page of your mind. Time quietly leaves the scene: wind skimming over the surface of the sea like an infinity net, looping your breath to its rock face with a single monochromatic brushstroke. I extend my hand. Try to touch his darkness. Don't cry for the moon, he says. I climb the rainbow into the night and reach for a web of stars. Take a leap of faith and fall in a poem that reminds me of *Wuthering Heights*. I hear you calling. Feel the formlessness of the wind scratch my heart, unwinding its chambers and tributaries. I drink the moon dry.

Ariadne Dreams of a New Relativity

Pitch black. No water. The monster's breath is cold and smells of carrion. Always in debt, once bankrupted, arrested and imprisoned, now he's in hiding. Although he roars and curses and says the universe is but a huge expletive, I'm not scared (been there before.) *Shh. Shh. Shh.* Think of the metaphysical implications of black holes, dark matter, the big bang and string theory. We could expand the Labyrinth with a slew of metaphors. Slay all the fake gods of Logos, purge their purgatories, destroy Limbo and generate new galaxies where you could hear the light. Touch God's parched skin. Grind Time's bristles. Wring Death's neck. Galaxies where shooting stars would surge and rush, swell and fall. Now, give me a rope. Let's sing to the glory of the Minotaur.

Archives of the Future

After Oscar Dominguez

Stench of the born-again wild beast slouching towards infinity. The horizon spouts clouds. Your typewriter and its neuron words settle on time's cleft. Craters rise to the skies, witnesses to history's expunged signs.

In the beginning you imagined cold air on skin, white gloves, pencil, paper. Enlisted words undercutting representation's factual value. But people are ever puppets on strings held by ungloved hands. They leap out of musty pages, return you to *arkhē*'s suffixal form, *arkheion*. Skip the record of a lifetime's metaphors, wielding words from the paterfamilias' house, to unanimous chorus, to Law Court.

The body's storehouse gathers abjection's silt; it is the cave where defiance buried you alive—call it Thebes, Bedlam, Holloway, or Other. It is where duty and language never collide with memory on your sister's lips. Yet words are not bats to be released from caves. They are birds set free from cages to open the heart's secret chambers. Inviolate, they are open to revision, still. See how they spread their wings. How high they soar.

Cross-swell Heisenberg

Sky shot with stars. A heartbeat. The water's edge is shrouded in fog. The sea is butterfly bones soaking in moon loom frizz. Crackling breeze. A whale cries out. You sit right on the edge of the cliff like you are Shelley, hair floating algae, air shocked out of your lungs. A brinkness. About face. Whitecaps fume and flicker. Rollers gush. Break. Stones flip up on the shore. A cavernous ribbed ragged *Schaumkrone* leaf wave rises up to the white horse moon. Thunder. Flash of light. Rain. Dappled grey nightmare. The mare rears. Kicks. It's an emergency metaphor. A catachresis made flesh. Hailstones. A piano mannequin lolls in the tide. Washes up. Unshackles. Her face is a tidal luminescence. The waves run away from the storm. Pomegranates explode. Glass skittles along the coral reef-ish shoreline. Everything from green to the outer edges of violet catches on fire. Between us, flitting flies glitter. A song breaks. It's a cavalcade of giraffes: *Gravida*.

Aseptic Perception

I extinguish those go get eyes. Welcome a winged victory. I want to believe there is an absence of hate love in this pandemonium. This blue pestilence. This soaked paper aeroplane with a broken wing grounded for all eternity next to the angel of history. They macerate in octopus ink, the plane and the angel. Sombre tones seep through the monochromatic scheme only a maniac could have devised. A paranoiac godlet from IMAGING, says something spawned by *Les Chants de Maldoror*, a reverie that moves associatively and appositionally to cover and uncover the most extravagant images and proclamations of abjection. Say it! Declare imminent hostilities. Grill some brains with mashed sardines and anchovies. Char us, squashed as we are in this corset you call a room when we are meant to explore the limits of painting. Assassinate poetry. Resurrect prose. Only to describe, define and affirm the visible. *Portray*. No. Poetic physiology is not the physiology of living creatures, although minds unmind after blasted hearts. Nothing is *d'après nature*. Eat that nothing mixed with blitzed green chilli, coriander, lime juice, olive oil, absinth. See what I destroyed. Taste what I did mean.

Twinklewinkalling

Lilac and jasmine in the air. Indigo. Violet light of a grave-lit moon. Black motes swirl in iridescent blue. Whirl, twirl and settle on your name. Jay—from the Latin for Gaea. You always wanted to fly, but have been grounded a lifetime. God knows I tried to change the script. I look for all *twinklewinkalling* gone. A Rorschach is what you left. Cold blade lips. A palimpsest of bruises. Vacated are your emerald eyes. Winter is in your mouthless mouth. I imagine your dreams, realities, nightmares, suffocations. Once you told me in your waking life you flew. Despite the grounding. How you feared falling off bridges. It was vertigo and agoraphobia took your breath away. No angel wings here, although they say they are always blue. How many times can you die? I zero in on the white hole of the question mark. No breath. Your throat, cinereous grey, is lined with needles. A thimbleful of bluish light. A chrysalis. Cells twitch, uncurl, zizz out. Fizz beyond imaging, beyond the apocalypse of bloods and tissues, beyond the wildest imaginings. A noose dangles, lonely; motes whirl in the luminescence of day—a drama you staged in air and liquid desire for your solitary pleasure.

Ekphrastic Still

These walls are made of language as tough as granite. We built them together word by word, syllable by monosyllable, letter by letter. Scraped them clean of dreams after you'd spent all our love on the irreal real. I stole all the rhymes, assonances, alliterations, intervals, elisions and silences to get you back. But you spread *crépi* all over the concrete and I stuck little barbs and hooks in it as it dried. I swore to have these walls ruined. Even drew up plans. The first part of the scheme was the Poeisis Tower. It was designed for use without melting clocks. You packed it with biblical and medieval iconography. So, I splashed mortar all over. Stuck a sign saying FOR RESTORATION and ran away before succumbing to your murderous fantasies. A great loss to the history of craftsmanship, but a tribute to the unfinished story of *l'Amur*. I should have considered the possibility of a Real Staircase emulating Late Lacanian Baroque.

Con Brio

After Antonio Vivaldi, Venice 1678 - Vienna 1741

I want it alive. Hold my breath. Summon my instrument. The marvellous pharynx at the top and back of my throat throbs in my mind's eye. I see the constrictors, muscles of the soft palate and eustachian tubes that connect the top of my throat to the middle ear. I hear you say in my head *buccinator, mandible, orbicularis oris*. Taste the words. Swallow. Breathe in. Pull in my cheeks and lash out at Vivaldi's clamorous, insistent, racing strings: ***Se lento encora il fulmine***. The air ignites. I am the Big Bang. The birth of the world. My own birth. Duplicitous Argippo's death. I come alive inside and outside the cascade that fills the stage. My voice booms. EX-**plodes**. OVER-**flows**. Drowns Vivaldi's strings. Drowns ARGH-**ippo**. Death to geminate faced Argippo whose love was many of its own kind. **BOOM! KA-BOOM!** Death to all cunning bastards! The pharynx at the top and back of my throat throbs. Constricts. Unties. The rage of all women roars in this single voice in the da capo: ***SE LENTO ENCORA IL FULMINE.***

Viz. Argippo, *Dramma per Musica, Libretto da Domenico Lalli, Atto Primo.*

How It Is

It was the end of a summer day on the bus where a little girl, or was it a boy, rocked their Barbie doll and I, a sitting figurine in decomposition, had no word to describe the light, the sky's absolute perfection and the wheels of the clouds going *round and round, round and round*. Just as one presumes that paradise exists, one assumes that reality exists. The reality of the clouds high above the mountain. The foothills and escarpments covered in trees and not at all bare as I would have drawn them had you asked me to *Plea-ease* draw me a mountain with a sheep atop. A light between sky and clouds and mountain. A Jurassic light. A flicks and dinosaurs kind of light. The diplodocus neck of the light with the sky its absolutely perfect skeleton. I didn't want to know the first word I'd say after you'd left. I wanted to live in real time with the summer you and the clouds going *round and round, round and round* and the wind going *swish* and *swish* in real light outside the bus.

Champagne Supernova, *Taché*

Starlight, annular. Self-luminous and thermonuclear coils in a nest. Shot silk. Alive taffeta. Scales, feathers, down, fur, skin. Pinkish brightening against the jet-black sky. Implosion. Compression. Explosion. Spicules. Your eyes, red-rimmed, hurt with gaseous light unlighting. Spectroscopic pulsation of pinks and reds. Slow whirl of carmine, vermillion, *giroflée,* red lead, scarlet pink, fuchsia, baby pink, rust-speckled traces of brain matter. Swirling cloud of hydrogen, helium, carbon, neon, oxygen, silicon. You plunge into your own dismembering body. Rise up to the surface. Cool down. Plunge again, *inwardoutward*. Cicadas scurry through your *bodymindsoul*, carnation-darnation chills. You breathe in tantric fashion when what you need is an antipyretic, analgesic, emetic. *Pfffff*... Fast slow entropy. Hundreds of billions of years in three little seconds, snuffed. Three caskets in stellar atmosphere. No, Doctor, this is no hallucination. *This is the* real real. Life leaches away from you. Tubular bells. Church quiet. A whiff of incense and black sun. *The world's still spinning round, we don't know why... Gegenschein.* Light curve. Crepuscular rays. Green flash. Twinkle. You sail ahead of *timenotime* into the dark bubbling out of gravitas. Radiate your own heat. Blow apart in a brilliant anti-anthropic stellar body dispersing on the other side of the eclipsing pillars of creation, purple lake, ultra-deep charcoal shades. The Dead Sea *Asphaltum*. Stardust, afloat.

Whimsical

We are polishing our *Once and Well* chardy under a silver wattle bursting forth in millions of golden blossoms at Hanging Rock when we notice a track leading into the forest. We follow it past clumps of stringy barks and peppermint gums as it winds beside the river dappled with late winter light. Warm wind gusts from up the gully. Thin stalks of grass billow like your bald man's comb-over. We marvel at the large multi-branched trees with smooth white bark shedding in curling ribbons, dense spreading crowns of long narrow leaves, rough barked trunks underneath. You joke that manna gums are notorious for dropping large limbs. Yes, often fatal, I riposte. We push on, stamping our feet on the leaf-littered dry, not noticing the clouds of gnats hovering in the air, the tiny swooping ravens. There is a chill in the air. We stumble on an old hollow tree quartering an army of gnomes, some bearded, some bald, but mostly clean-shaven as if ready for a hard day's work. *Hey ho. Hey ho.* Carved on the hollow's lip is a sign: GNOME SWEET GNOME. We chuckle. Take a closer look at the little fellows. So sweet, you say, in a surreal way. I dunno; they look… I say, trailing on a word's shadow—sinister. Nah, it's a lovely whimsical thing. A snort. I'm an old friend, says the wind, softly. Then screams: Kill them.

The Edge Land of Daydreams

I've never counted the bones in my hand, but I have an extra finger shaped like a honey eater's beak—an esoteric bit of fleshed-out bone that blocks all light except the liquid bandwidth emitted by ionised hydrogen in burning honey that reveals the cloying structures of gas corralled by magnetic fields and birds of paradise. My extra finger enables me to feel the inside of blackwood buds. Taste the nectar of their nebulae-filled umbraphile flowers. Smell the heat of what will be called this year's hydrogen alpha bee bushfire. See the next total eclipse of the sun at Exmouth. Capture the cosmic inferno that will be known in one thousand and one nights. The mother of utter silence.

Unwrite the "I" from the poem.

Mid-walk, the skies open. Rain pours. Yellow water rises, swirling about, soon gushing out of the broken creek's banks, carving furrows among grass, reeds, bushes and trees. The dog takes the lead and pins us to the bridge. Murky calm where the path tilts and narrows. Here, the water curves and swerves in its own bed, pulls at silt. The current pushes it out unseen, against the sunken stepping stones. Here, the water swirls, froths, falls and rushes towards the edge land of daydreams. Towards the immargination of the page.

Rrose Sélavy

C'est moi, said Marcel Duchamp, my cross-dressed body transfigured into readymade in furs—almost femme fatale, lipsticked and bejewelled, intent on luring Man Ray and André Breton like some erotic algorithm, uncanny signature pointing to the gap between ego and alter, retinal and anti. Such art—or is she merely oxymoronic, already fetishized?

Rrose's own preference, never for binary programs nudges up through one hundred years of seeming oblivion in the dim lights of libraries, studios, art catalogues.

How sharp the eyes in the averted gaze said an angel with horns called René Magritte, thus signing Rrose's enucleation with the stroke of a memorable apocryphal phrase.

Letter to a Bride to Be

Thank you for sharing with me the newest (yet quite retro) issue of *Vogue Bridal Patterns*. I love that off-white shot silk you brought back from your travels and think it would suit your complexion perfectly. It looks much better than the Nora white organza. It's also a tribute to your integrity and I hope I'm not reading too much into your choice of colour. But before you start making the dress, I urge you to indulge in a little intertextual journey around your maiden room, if I may say so, for I'm not sure you know on what *galère* you are embarking. Mark my words. I don't mean *gondola*, or anything romantic, but *galley*, a low, flat ship with one or more sails (glad you opted for a visor instead of a veil) and up to three banks of oars worked by slaves. First, as an artist, you must re-read Tennyson's *The Lady of Shalott* against the grain. Then turn to Elizabeth Bishop's *The Gentleman of Shalott* and Jessica Anderson's *Tirra Lirra by the River*. I studied both in year twelve (wish I'd paid more attention.) Finally, and this may surprise you, especially coming from me, read Henrik Ibsen's *A Doll House*, a work your father drew on to devise our home. Deep down, I now think Ibsen understood the difference between need and desire; desire and love; love and lust. Your father would disagree, of course, but I would maintain that Ibsen was really a proto-feminist writer. *Wink*. One last thing: beware of identifications. With two (anti)heroines bearing your Christian name, you wouldn't want to become unduly hystericized.

Magritte's Gravestone

draws on the *faculty which perceives at once, quite without resort to philosophic methods, the intimate and secret connections between things, correspondences and analogies* from Baudelaire to Lautréamont to Breton to Magritte, who *used to provoke ... shock by causing the encounter of unrelated objects.* It would have to be called *Elective Affinities,* after a novel by Goethe. So, just as an image results from preliminary *investigations and accidental encounters*—say a bicycle & a cigar or a cigar & a fish (with smoke curling and swirling up) at the *intersection* of a paradoxical *synthesis of antithetical concepts* or *interpenetrating images*, the poem is *tacitly comprised of objects that remain to be found.* Think of *The Seducer* (1950), where *the sea takes the form of a ship,* or authorised *Plagiarism* (1960), where *a bouquet on a table has been replaced by the landscape outside.* In this painting the antithetical concepts 'inside' and 'outside' (or 'here' and 'there') have been synthesized in a single image, but they are also still understood as two images by the mind as are three perfect eggs in a nest.

This sentence waits to migrate past the confines of the page. It's moonstruck. Watch its metamorphosis.

Ceci n'est pas une pipe: we are made of letters. Look how they liquefy in the inkpot.

A Haunting

Wading into fallen stars that stream towards the mouth of forgetting as surely as Heinrich von Kleist's self-appointed gun you catch a glimpse of my mask, Orpheus. It is red like a child's first blood. It smells of wattle, musk and frangipani. It sounds like mirrors smashing shadows, although the moon is high and full of Dürer's kinetic hues. As the curtain of the archive of the world of the living lifts, your anamorphic skull comes into view. In that hypnagogic instant I catch a glimpse of the heart from which I'll die: it is surrounded by swans taking on the hour's changing colours. Feel fluff, plumes, feathers, quills, barbs, spines, spikes. I think of Dalí's aphasic metaphors. Hear Kandinsky's asphyxiated screams. Wait for your otherworldly cry. It is like crystal shattering one thousand and one nights from before the invention of the word plumage and it does not end. D minor. *Crescendo.*

Less Is a Bore

The house, a Multiplex hologram, stands against the wind, facing the fallen world at Chestnut Hill, Philadelphia. The façade evokes a child's picture of a Georgian mansion: arch above the doorway, lintel coursing through it, gable recalling a classical pediment. It is split at the apex, suggesting the brokenness of time and home. The crossed-out window to your left is a pastiche of Mondrian's *The Kiss*. It celebrates architecture as art. Opening into new realms of creation. The strip windows at your right express the man child's desire to move out. The house is like a poem. It conjures up the human need for stimulation, surprise, change. Its vocabulary is eclectic, inventive. Inside there are no curtains, no blinds blocking out the world. The studio, where some of this world swings by for a chat, a drink, a laugh, I call contingent. Here, among yuccas, orchids, bonsais and African violets, I mess with words, lines, shapes, structures, images, rhythms, textures. This is where poems, drawings, paintings, sculptures, maquettes and garments evolve, intertwining time and space under the piercing gaze of Antonin Artaud.

π

A whiff of butter, caramel, French fries and booze in the air that swells in the city's cooing clamour. Voiceless, you follow your feet. Up and up they climb the bumpy cobbled streets towards the medieval castle's remains. All around, the walls of the old town radiate heat. Up they walk you, your feet, to the tipping point of the landscape. They take you to Villa Noailles. Closing time. You sit down on a garden bench. Your parched skin soaks in stray droplets of water from the sprinklers. You wonder what time they close the gate. Notice the height of the iron fence.

She arrives the way birds do. Soundlessly. Fleetingly. Drinking the air. Irony in her gaze. She perches next to you. Unties your tongue: π, you say, don't mind me I'm only gathering fragments of living.

π laughs. Asks if you've been to the salt marshes on the Giens peninsula. Says she loves waterbirds. That you should go to Porquerolles; walk the rocky trails and snorkel in the *criques* for they are full of underwater shipwrecks. This would suit you, who inhabits no space, but time's broken line.

Vous n'êtes pas très loquace, says π in this strange tongue full of understatements, reiterations, reproaches; this plu-perfect tongue that once allowed you to renounce what might have been.

It's November, or June. *Hier.* Her name is Prose or Rose. *Papier buvard* of bygone times. Blotting paper. Drinking paper. Avid. And I, emptying. Already empty. *Vide.* Blotted out. How words climb back time and give way to what can only be encountered one step at a time.

Words shot with odours of butter and caramel, echoes, sensations. Melting moments. And now this bird woman with a tongue as sharp as a blade who converses silently with magpies and blackbirds in the brokenness of time. Hyères, between dog and wolf. Anything could happen.

Telescopic

A knock on the door. How could that be at a time of confinement? Normally you would peek through the curtains, but now that all glass has been replaced by tightly fitting stainless-steel windows you're caught at your own game, Professor. *Knock. Knock. Knock.* A glance at the computer screen. You should be worried, you know. For decades you've been knocking on the door of civil and military space agencies, trying to get access to sounding rockets and satellites because in your eyes space has theoretical as well as technical advantages such as the absence of gravity and low level of thermal perturbations. Feel how cold the house is. How it begins to rock. And look: your telescope's marching across the room now, its big eye fastened on you.

Endgame with No Ending

You too once thought you were on top of your game. After the Titans of the University were defeated, you shared a hot desk on Mount Olympus with astronomists and astrophysicists who, unlike you, conducted their collaborative research behind the closed doors of their laboratories. Every third Friday of the month you would meet at the Pantheon, the space where all the vigorous discussions among the scientists and chief administrators took place. Then one fateful morning you packed your meagre pack of books and moved to the foot of Mount Parnassus (the handful of linguists and historians and philosophers had long disappeared.) Having embraced the principle of heterogeneity inscribed within the very ethos of Parnassus, you devoted yourself to a theatre of dreams, visions, mirrors, smokescreens and metaphors where images replace imitations that generate specular emotional responses in a constant act of deconstruction to reveal the core of an encounter of self with other. Now you exhume your life on the sTREEt OF croCODiIES. Cymbals!

Notes

The epigraph is taken from Jonathan Foer's *Tree of Codes*, Visual Editions, 2010, p. 92, with gaps approximating the original.

Anaphora takes its title from Elizabeth Bishop's poem of the same name. The opening line echoes Bishop's first two lines.

The italicised phrase in *The Entombment* is sourced from Coleridge's 'Kubla Khan'.

Borges and I refers to one of Jorge Luis Borges' famous parables published in the collection *Labyrinths*, Penguin, 1970, pp. 282-83.

Archives of the Future is an ekphrastic response to Oscar Dominguez's 1938 oil painting *Lembranca do Futuro* (*Memory of the Future*) which hangs at the Tenerife Espacio de las Artes, Spain. The poem's opening stanza focuses on a detail in the upper left corner. There is an obvious allusion to W. B. Yeats's 'The Second Coming' in lines 1-2 to convey a sense of anxiety about the future.

Ekphrastic Still: l'amur' is a Lacanian pun melding 'amour' / 'love' and 'mur' / wall. The capitalisation of the term in the piece is an ironic spin on Lacan's own term to suggest that *l'amur* is on the side of the Symbolic.

How It Is: the phrase 'Sitting figure in decomposition' alludes to Dalí's *Kneeling Figure in Decomposition* (1950) housed at The Salvador Dalí Museum, St Petersburg, Florida.

Champagne Supernova, Taché: 'The world's still spinning round, we don't know why' and part of the title are taken from the song 'Champagne Supernova' by Oasis.

Magritte's Gravestone: the first part of this piece is lifted or manipulated from Suzi Gablik's *Magritte*, Thames & Hudson, 1976, pp. 102-108.

Less Is a Bore: It is the American architect Robert Venturi who coined the phrase 'less is a bore'. This prose poem draws on a photograph of the house he designed for his mother.

Endgame with No Ending: The title of Jonathan Foer's *Tree of Codes* exhumes and manipulates *The Street of Crocodiles*, a book by Bruno Schultz. In fact, as Foer tells us in an afterword, *Tree of Codes* is 'a die-cut book by erasure' of Schultz' work (Foer, 2010, 138).

Selected Poetry Titles Published by SurVision Books

Seeds of Gravity: An Anthology of Contemporary Surrealist Poetry from Ireland
Edited by Anatoly Kudryavitsky
ISBN 978-1-912963-18-8

Invasion: An Anthology of Ukrainian Poetry about the War
Edited by Tony Kitt
ISBN 978-1-912963-32-4

Noelle Kocot. *Humanity*
(New Poetics: USA)
ISBN 978-1-9995903-0-7

Marc Vincenz. *Einstein Fledermaus*
(New Poetics: USA)
ISBN 978-1-912963-20-1

Helen Ivory. *Maps of the Abandoned City*
(New Poetics: England)
ISBN 978-1-912963-04-1

Tony Kitt. *The Magic Phlute*
(New Poetics: Ireland)
ISBN 978-1-912963-08-9

John W. Sexton. *Inverted Night*
(New Poetics: Ireland)
ISBN 978-1-912963-05-8

Afric McGlinchey. *Invisible Insane*
(New Poetics: Ireland)
ISBN 978-1-9995903-3-8

Michelle Moloney King. *Another Word for Mother*
(New Poetics: Ireland)
ISBN 978-1-912963-31-7

Matthew Geden. *Fruit*
(New Poetics: Ireland)
ISBN 978-1-912963-16-4

Clayre Benzadón. *Liminal Zenith*
(New Poetics: USA)
ISBN 978-1-912963-11-9

Thomas Townsley. *Tangent of Ardency*
(New Poetics: USA)
ISBN 978-1-912963-15-7

Mikko Harvey & Jake Bauer. *Idaho Falls*
(Winner of James Tate Poetry Prize 2018)
ISBN 978-1-912963-02-7

Tony Bailie. *Mountain Under Heaven*
(Winner of James Tate Poetry Prize 2019)
ISBN 978-1-912963-09-6

Charles Kell. *Pierre Mask*
(Winner of James Tate Poetry Prize 2019)
ISBN 978-1-912963-19-5

Jon Riccio. *Eye, Romanov*
(Winner of James Tate Poetry Prize 2020)
ISBN 978-1-912963-24-9

Aoife Mannix. *Alice under the Knife*
(Winner of James Tate Poetry Prize 2020)
ISBN 978-1-912963-26-3

Alison Dunhill. *As Pure as Coal Dust*
(Winner of James Tate Poetry Prize 2020)
ISBN 978-1-912963-23-2

Charles Borkhuis. *Spontaneous Combustion*
(Winner of James Tate Poetry Prize 2021)
ISBN 978-1-912963-30-0

Noah Falck and Matt McBride. *Prerecorded Weather*
(Winner of James Tate Poetry Prize 2022)
ISBN 978-1-912963-39-3

Michael Zeferino Spring. *Kahlo's Window*
(Winner of James Tate Poetry Prize 2022)
ISBN 978-1-912963-40-9

Ciaran O'Driscoll. *Angel Hour*
ISBN 978-1-912963-27-0

Tim Murphy. *The Mouth of Shadows*
ISBN 978-1-912963-29-4

George Kalamaras. *That Moment of Wept*
ISBN 978-1-9995903-7-6

George Kalamaras. *Through the Silk-Heavy Rains*
ISBN 978-1-912963-28-7

Anton G. Leitner. *Selected Poems 1981–2015*
Translated from German
ISBN 978-1-9995903-8-3

Order our books from http://survisionmagazine.com/bookshop.htm

www.ingramcontent.com/pod-product-compliance
Lightning Source LLC
Chambersburg PA
CBHW061312040426
42444CB00010B/2605